This book belongs to:

____

24 23 22 21 1 2 3 4

Published by Tughra Books
335 Clifton Ave.
Clifton, NJ, 07011, USA
www.tughrabooks.com

ISBN: 979-8-89729-504-3

Mini Muslims Series ISBN 9781597849692

WHO ARE Muslims?

Muslims believe and submit to God.

Allah is the One True God.

Muslims believe in all of Allah's angels, books, and prophets.

Allah is the Creator of everything.

Allah is the Most Kind and Most Powerful.

Muslims obey Him and follow His prophets.

Muslims believe in the Quran.
The Quran is Allah’s words that
He sent down to Prophet Muhammad (pbuh)
to teach us how to live.

Muslims do good. They tell the truth, take care of others, help the needy, stand up for what is right, and stop what is wrong.

We love being

Muslim!

I ♥
Being Muslim